ADHD Wife

Supporting Your ADHD Partner In Navigating Life and Marriage With ADHD

Doreen C Davis

Table of Contents

"Your ADHD is a part of who you are, but it doesn't define you. You are so much more than your diagnosis, and you have the power to create a life filled with joy, purpose, and success."

In this book, we will explore the effects that ADHD can have on a wife and her non-ADHD husband, and provide practical strategies and coping mechanisms to help manage these challenges. We will also discuss the importance of educating others and raising awareness about ADHD, in order to reduce stigma and promote understanding.

I never knew that I had ADHD until later in life. Growing up, I always knew that I was a little different from my peers, but I never quite understood why. I struggled with organization, time management, cooking, and almost all the things women are supposed to be naturally good at. I often felt like I was playing catch-up. Despite these challenges, I was able to get through school and even landed a good job after graduation. But things started to change when I got married.

My husband was organized, detail-oriented, and always on top of things. He was my perfect complement, and I loved him for it. However, I couldn't help but feel like I was letting him down in some way. I would forget important dates, misplace important documents, and struggle to keep up with the demands of daily life.

I knew that I needed to do something, but I didn't know what. I started to research my symptoms and stumbled upon ADHD.

Suddenly, everything started to make sense. The constant distractions, the inability to focus, the impulsivity, it all clicked. I made an appointment with a specialist and was officially diagnosed with ADHD.

At first, I felt overwhelmed and even a little ashamed. I felt like I had been hiding a part of myself for so long and now everyone knew. But as I began to learn more about ADHD, I realized that it wasn't a weakness, but rather a unique way of thinking and processing information.

I started to understand that my brain was wired differently and that it was okay.

With my diagnosis, I was finally able to get the help that I needed. I started managing it and working with a therapist to learn new coping strategies. My husband was incredibly supportive throughout the process, and I felt like we were finally on the same page. Now, I still have my moments where I forget things or get easily distracted, but I know how to manage them.

I have a better understanding of my strengths and weaknesses, and I'm able to communicate more effectively with my husband. I'm grateful for my ADHD diagnosis, as it has freed me from the shame and confusion that I once felt. I now embrace my unique perspective and look forward to what the future holds.

Through personal stories, expert insights, and evidence-based research, we will delve into the various ways that ADHD can impact a marriage, including communication breakdowns, difficulty with organization and time management, and struggles with emotional regulation. We will also provide tips for managing these issues, including lifestyle changes, therapy, medication, and other treatments.

By reading this book, you will gain a greater understanding of ADHD and its impact on marriage, as well as practical tools and techniques to help you and your spouse manage the challenges that may arise. Whether you are a wife with ADHD or a non-ADHD husband, this book will provide valuable insights and strategies for navigating this condition and building a stronger, more resilient relationship.

Chapter One:What is ADHD

ADHD (Attention-Deficit/Hyperactivity Disorder) is a neurodevelopmental disorder that affects both children and adults. People with ADHD typically have difficulties with paying attention, hyperactivity, and impulsivity. The symptoms of ADHD can vary from person to person and can cause significant impairment in social, academic, and occupational functioning.

There Are Three Subtypes of ADHD:

Inattentive type (formerly known as ADD): characterized by difficulties with attention, focus, organization, and follow-through on tasks.

Hyperactive-impulsive type: characterized by hyperactivity, impulsivity, restlessness, and difficulty waiting their turn.

Combined type: characterized by symptoms of both inattention and hyperactivity/impulsivity.

ADHD is typically diagnosed by a mental health professional such as a psychiatrist or a clinical psychologist, based on a thorough evaluation of the individual's symptoms, medical history, and behavioural observations. Treatment options for ADHD may include medication, behavioural therapy, or a combination of both.

Self Screening Assessment

If you think that you have ADHD, there are screening tools online to start with. It is important to note that while tests can be useful screening tools, they do not provide a definitive diagnosis of ADHD. Only a qualified healthcare professional, such as a psychologist or psychiatrist, can diagnose ADHD. Women are as prone to ADHD as men, and the struggle with the symptoms is unending. Women are more prone to emotional imbalance, and ADHD worsens it. The good news is you can overcome your most frustrating symptoms of ADHD with more tailored assistance.

The most common test for ADHD is the Adult ADHD Self-Report Scale (ASRS-v1.1). This is a screening tool designed to identify symptoms of ADHD in adults. It consists of 18 questions that cover the two main symptom clusters of ADHD: inattention and hyperactivity/impulsivity.

Another widely used test is the Conners' Adult ADHD Rating Scale (CAARS). The CAARS is a comprehensive assessment tool that evaluates a range of ADHD symptoms, including inattention, hyperactivity, impulsivity, and other associated features such as anxiety and depression.

Other attitude tests for ADHD include the Barkley Adult ADHD Rating Scale (BAARS), the Wender Utah Rating Scale (WURS), and the Brown Attention-Deficit Disorder Scale (BADDS). These tests are often used in combination with clinical interviews and observations to provide a more complete picture of an individual's ADHD symptoms and their impact on daily functioning.

Chapter Two:Supporting your ADHD partner

Caring for a spouse with ADHD can be challenging at times, but with patience and understanding, you can create a supportive and loving environment that can help your wife manage her symptoms. Here are some tips that may be helpful:

Learn about ADHD: Educate yourself about the condition and how it affects your wife. Understanding the symptoms and challenges of ADHD can help you be more patient and supportive.

Communicate effectively: Communication is key in any relationship, and it is especially important when one partner has ADHD. Try to be clear, direct, and specific when communicating with your wife. Avoid being critical or judgmental, and encourage open and honest communication.

Create structure and routine: People with ADHD often struggle with organization and time management. Creating structure and routine can be helpful in managing these challenges. Develop a schedule together and use tools such as calendars, timers, and to-do lists to help your wife stay on track.

Be patient and understanding: People with ADHD may struggle with impulsivity, distractibility, and forgetfulness. It is important to be patient and understanding when your wife experiences these symptoms. Avoid taking her behaviour personally and try to be supportive and encouraging.

Keep in mind that both partners should take responsibility for their challenges in a relationship. It's not your job to change your partner, but you can assist them in managing their traits and behaviours. Encourage and offer positive feedback to support their efforts. By gaining knowledge about adult ADHD, you can better understand your partner's perspective and develop greater compassion and tolerance.

Take care of yourself: Caring for a spouse with ADHD can be challenging and may take a toll on your well-being. It is important to take care of yourself as well. Make sure to get enough rest, exercise, and social support.

Remember, ADHD is a condition that your wife has, not who she is. With your support and understanding, she can manage her symptoms and lead a happy and fulfilling life

Does Your Wife Ever?

These are simply a series of questions aimed at identifying whether your partner or someone close to you might have ADHD. If you or someone you know relates to some of the questions asked, it may be worth considering taking an ADHD screening test.

Does she often write shopping lists but forget to bring them to the market?

Does she have a habit of forgetting to put things back where they belong?

Does she frequently forget anniversaries and birthdays?

Is she always seeking more adventure, even in the bedroom?

Does she tend to zone out during conversations with her spouse?

Is she consistently late and struggles with punctuality?

Does she tend to start many businesses with plenty of ideas, but fail to follow through on them?

Does she occasionally pick fights just because she's bored?

Does she stumble on the clutter that she created?

Does she frequently meet people in the wrong place?

Does she make lots of plans without actually following through with them?

Does she often fail to listen when spoken to directly?

Does she have a habit of blurting out answers before a question has been completed?

Does she recall random facts from the past but struggle to remember what she did yesterday?

Does she interrupt or intrude on others frequently?

Does she fidget frequently, have difficulty completing tasks or following through on plans, and have difficulty shifting attention?

Does she excessively shift from one activity to another, have difficulty concentrating on reading, and display impatience?

Is she frequently preoccupied with her thoughts and fails to hear others when spoken to?

Does she have trouble sitting still and engaging in sudden and unexpected mood swings?

Does she interrupt conversations and speak without considering the consequences?

Does she have a hot temper and a need for high stimulus?

Does she struggle with forgetfulness and have a low tolerance for frustration?

Does she tend toward substance abuse?

Does she exhibit a high burst of energy?

Does she demonstrate laser focus on things she enjoys?

Does she find it challenging to clean?"

Chapter Three: Causes of ADHD in Women

The exact causes of ADHD in women are not completely understood. However, there is likely to be a combination of genetic and environmental factors that contribute to the development of the disorder.

Here are some factors that are believed to play a role in the development of ADHD in women:

Genetics: ADHD has been shown to have a strong genetic component, with studies indicating that genes may account for up to 70-80% of the risk for the disorder. Women who have a family history of ADHD are more likely to develop the condition themselves.

Hormonal factors: Hormones, particularly estrogen, may play a role in the development of ADHD in women. Research suggests that hormonal changes during puberty, menstruation, pregnancy and menopause may contribute to the development or worsening of symptoms.

Brain structure and function: Studies have shown that there are differences in the structure and function of the brains of individuals with ADHD and that these differences may be more pronounced in women. Research has also suggested that women with ADHD may have less activity in the prefrontal cortex, which is part of the brain responsible for impulse control and decision-making.

Environmental factors: Environmental factors, such as exposure to toxins or stress, may also play a role in the development of ADHD. Some studies have suggested that maternal stress during pregnancy or exposure to lead or other toxins may increase the risk of developing ADHD.

It's important to note that ADHD can be difficult to diagnose in women, as symptoms may present differently than in men or boys. Women with ADHD may be more likely to experience inattentive symptoms rather than hyperactive or impulsive symptoms, which may lead to underdiagnosis or misdiagnosis. If you suspect that you or someone you know may have ADHD, it's important to seek a professional diagnosis and appropriate treatment.

Chapter Four:Symptoms of ADHD in Women

Inattention: Women with ADHD may struggle with paying attention to details, organizing tasks and activities, or following through on tasks.

Hyperactivity: While hyperactivity is more commonly associated with ADHD in boys and men, women with ADHD may also experience restlessness, fidgeting, or difficulty staying still.

Difficulty with organization and time management: Women with ADHD often struggle to keep track of schedules and deadlines, and may have difficulty organizing their thoughts or completing tasks.

Poor memory: Women with ADHD may struggle with forgetfulness, including difficulty remembering details or important events.

Difficulty with focusing or concentrating: Women with ADHD may find it hard to stay focused on tasks or may be easily distracted by external stimuli. This can make their partner feel ignored, especially if the individual's ADHD is undiagnosed. Without an explanation for this distraction, the non-ADHD partner might misinterpret the behaviour as a lack of care and concern.

Impulsivity: Women with ADHD may act impulsively or have difficulty controlling their behaviour or emotions, which can lead to problems in relationships and at work.

Emotional dysregulation: Women with ADHD may experience intense emotions or mood swings, and may have difficulty regulating their emotional responses to situations.

Restlessness: Women with ADHD may feel restless, constantly moving or fidgeting, and may have trouble sitting still.

Sensitivity to criticism: Women with ADHD may be more sensitive to criticism, and may struggle with low self-esteem or negative self-talk.

Self-esteem: Women with ADHD may struggle with feelings of low self-esteem, frustration, and shame due to the difficulties they face in managing their symptoms.

Not all women with ADHD will experience all of these symptoms, and the severity of the symptoms can vary.

Chapter Five:Treatment Options for Women With ADHD?

There are several treatment options available for ADHD that can help individuals manage their symptoms and improve their quality of life. From medication to behavioral therapy, treatment plans for ADHD are typically personalized to meet the specific needs of each individual. In this book, we will discuss some of the most common ADHD treatment options available, their benefits, and how individuals with ADHD can work with healthcare professionals to find the right treatment plan for them.

Holistic Approach

While medication is the most common treatment for ADHD, some people may want to explore holistic approaches, including the use of herbs and tea, as part of their management plan.

It's important to note that there is limited scientific evidence to support the use of herbs and tea in treating ADHD. However, some people may find that these natural remedies provide additional support in managing their symptoms. It's important to consult with a healthcare provider before trying any new treatment, including herbal remedies.

Here are some herbs and teas that may be worth exploring:

Ginseng: Ginseng is an adaptogenic herb that may help improve focus and cognitive function. Some studies suggest that it may help alleviate symptoms of ADHD in children and adults.

Ginkgo biloba: Ginkgo biloba is another herb that may help improve cognitive function, including attention and memory. Some studies suggest that it may be beneficial for people with ADHD.

Chamomile: Chamomile is a soothing herb that may help promote relaxation and reduce anxiety. It may be helpful for people with ADHD who experience anxiety and difficulty sleeping.

Lemon balm: Lemon balm is a herb that may help reduce anxiety and improve mood. Some studies suggest that it may be beneficial for people with ADHD.

Green tea: Green tea contains caffeine, which can help improve focus and alertness. It also contains L-theanine, an amino acid that may help promote relaxation and reduce anxiety.

It's important to remember that herbs and tea should not replace conventional treatments for ADHD, such as medication and therapy. However, incorporating these natural remedies into your management plan may provide additional support in managing your symptoms.

Conventional Approach

The conventional approach to treating ADHD typically involves a combination of medication, therapy, and lifestyle changes.

Medication: The most common medications used to treat ADHD are stimulants, such as Ritalin, Adderall, and Concerta. These medications work by increasing the levels of dopamine and norepinephrine in the brain, which can improve focus, attention, and impulse control.

There are several types of medications used to treat ADHD, including:

Stimulants: These medications are the most commonly prescribed and have been shown to be effective in treating ADHD symptoms. Examples include methylphenidate (Ritalin, Concerta, Metadate, Focalin) and amphetamines (Adderall, Dexedrine).

Non-stimulants: These medications are an alternative for people who cannot tolerate or do not respond to stimulants. Examples include atomoxetine (Strattera), guanfacine (Intuniv), and clonidine (Kapvay).

Antidepressants: Some antidepressants, such as bupropion (Wellbutrin), can be used to treat ADHD symptoms in addition to depression.

It is important to note that medication should be prescribed and monitored by a qualified healthcare professional, such as a psychiatrist. The type of medication prescribed and the dosage will vary depending on individual circumstances and medical history. Additionally, medication should be used in combination with other treatments, such as behavioural therapy and lifestyle changes, for best results.

Cognitive-Behavioural Therapy

Cognitive-behavioural therapy (CBT) is a type of talk therapy that focuses on changing negative thought patterns and behaviours. The therapy is based on the idea that the way we think about things affects how we feel and behave, and that by changing our thoughts and behaviours, we can change how we feel.

Here's a general overview of how CBT works:

Assessment: The therapist will start by assessing your current situation, including your thoughts, feelings, and behaviours. They may also ask about your past experiences, relationships, and other factors that may be contributing to your current difficulties.

Goal setting: Once the therapist has a good understanding of your situation, they will work with you to set specific, achievable goals for therapy.

Identifying negative thought patterns: The therapist will help you identify negative thought patterns that may be contributing to your difficulties. These may include thoughts that are self-critical, irrational, or overly negative.

Challenging negative thoughts: Once negative thought patterns have been identified, the therapist will help you challenge and change them. This may involve examining the evidence for and against a particular thought, and developing more realistic and balanced ways of thinking.

Learning new behaviours: In addition to changing negative thoughts, CBT also focuses on changing behaviours that may be contributing to difficulties. The therapist may teach you new skills for managing stress, improving communication, or setting boundaries, for example.

Practice and feedback: CBT is a skills-based therapy, which means that much of the work is done outside of therapy sessions. You will be asked to practice new skills between sessions, and the therapist will provide feedback and guidance to help you continue to improve.

Review and reflection: Throughout therapy, you and the therapist will review progress towards your goals and make adjustments as needed. At the end of therapy, you will reflect on the progress you've made and plan for how to maintain gains in the future.

Overall, CBT is a structured, goal-oriented therapy that can help people make significant improvements in their mental health and well-being.

Diet and Supplements

Diet and supplements can also play a role in managing ADHD symptoms, but they should not be used as a standalone treatment. Here are some dietary and supplement strategies that may be helpful in managing ADHD symptoms:

Avoiding certain foods: Some research suggests that certain foods can worsen ADHD symptoms. These include sugary foods, processed foods, and foods with artificial colors and preservatives. It may be helpful to limit or avoid these foods in the diet.

Eating a balanced diet: Eating a balanced diet that includes plenty of fruits, vegetables, whole grains, and lean protein can help provide the nutrients necessary for healthy brain function.

Omega-3 fatty acid supplements: Omega-3 fatty acids, found in fatty fish like salmon, may help improve cognitive function and reduce inflammation in the brain. Supplements may be helpful for people who don't consume enough omega-3s in their diet.

Iron and magnesium supplements: Some research suggests that iron and magnesium may help manage ADHD symptoms. However, it's important to speak with a healthcare provider before taking supplements, as too many of these nutrients can be harmful.

It's important to note that dietary and supplement strategies should be used in combination with other treatments, such as medication and therapy, to effectively manage ADHD symptoms. Additionally, these strategies may not work for everyone, and it's important to speak with a healthcare provider before making any changes to your diet or supplement regimen.

Chapter Six:Tips For Improving Relationship

The key to improving your relationship is to prioritize the way you interact with each other rather than obsessing over individual responsibilities. Instead of tackling logistical problems, it's important to first work on strengthening your emotional connection.

Make sure to schedule time for activities that bring you both happiness, and not just for resolving issues. It can be taxing to break old habits, so remember to take breaks and enjoy each other's company along the way.

One possible response to this situation could be, "I understand that you're feeling lonely, and I want to make it up to you. Let's plan something special to do together, just the two of us."

By acknowledging your partner's feelings and suggesting a specific activity to do together, you can demonstrate your commitment to the relationship and show that you value their needs. This can help you both connect and strengthen your bond.

Another response from the Non-ADHD partner could be, "I'm feeling lonely lately because you've been preoccupied. Let's go out and do something together."

This is because it's usual for an ADHD spouse to be preoccupied with other things, and it's perfectly normal for a partner who doesn't have ADHD to feel abandoned and lonely.

When your partner invites you to do something together and mentions feeling lonely or neglected, it can be helpful to understand that these feelings may stem from your ADHD-related distractions. By agreeing to spend quality time together, you can both step away from any racing thoughts and work towards repairing and strengthening your relationship.

Remember that it is a two-person effort. Both partners need to take responsibility for their own issues. You are not responsible for changing your partner, but you can support their efforts to manage their traits and characteristics more effectively.

It's important to note that these habits and foibles can vary from person to person and may not apply to every individual with ADHD. Additionally, it's important to approach these habits with understanding and empathy rather than judgment or frustration, as they are often a result of the ADHD symptoms rather than a choice or personal failing.

Chapter Seven: Unconventional Way of Dealing With ADHD

Fidgeting seems to serve a productive purpose for people with ADHD. It may help their brains compensate for a sense of under stimulation, and there's some evidence that people with ADHD focus better when they fidget.

In other words, despite all the times people with ADHD are told they should just "sit still," their fidgety nature isn't necessarily "bad." They might be instinctively doing what's best for their brains and what will help them concentrate. But, that doesn't change the fact that their constant moving around can be distracting and even downright annoying for the people around them.

The solution is to find forms of fidgeting that aren't intrusive for other people who are trying to focus in their vicinity. Working at a standing desk, using a stress ball, or chewing gum, for example, can all provide outlets for fidgety ADHD energy while creating minimal bother in terms of noise or visual distraction for people nearby.

Chapter Eight: Effect Of ADHD In a Sexual Relationship

ADHD can affect sexual relationships in a variety of ways for both husbands and wives. Here are some potential ways ADHD can impact sexual relationships:

Women with ADHD may have difficulty focusing on the sexual experience or may act impulsively during sexual encounters. This can make it difficult to fully enjoy and engage in sexual activity.

Women with ADHD may have trouble remembering important details related to sex, such as birth control or scheduling time for intimacy.

Women with ADHD may experience hyperactivity or restlessness during sexual encounters, which can make it difficult to relax and enjoy the experience.

Communication is a key part of a healthy sexual relationship, and individuals with ADHD may struggle with communication due to difficulties with attention, impulsivity, or social skills.

Women with ADHD may experience intense emotions or mood swings, which can impact their sexual relationship with their partner.

There is no evidence to suggest that individuals with ADHD are more likely to cheat in a relationship or develop an addiction to porn than individuals without ADHD. It is important to recognize that ADHD is a neurological disorder that can impact an individual's ability to focus, organize, and manage impulsivity, but it does not determine an individual's morality or behaviour.

However, some individuals with ADHD may struggle with impulse control, leading to impulsive behaviours such as engaging in risky sexual behaviour and developing problematic patterns of pornography use. It's also possible that an individual with ADHD may struggle with communication or maintaining intimacy in a relationship, which could contribute to problems in the relationship.

How ADHD Affect Pregnant Wife

ADHD can potentially affect a pregnant woman in a few different ways, both in terms of her own health and the health of the developing fetus. Here are a few potential ways that ADHD can impact pregnancy:

Medication use: Many women with ADHD take medication to manage symptoms, but some ADHD medications may not be safe to take during pregnancy. A healthcare professional can help determine if medication is necessary, and if so, recommend a medication that is safe to take during pregnancy.

Increased stress: Women with ADHD may experience increased stress during pregnancy due to difficulties with organization, time management, and emotional regulation. This can potentially have negative effects on the developing fetus.

Increased risk of preterm birth: Some studies have found that women with ADHD may be at increased risk for preterm birth, potentially due to the physiological effects of stress and anxiety on the body.

Increased risk of preeclampsia: Preeclampsia is a condition that can develop during pregnancy and can potentially be more common in women with ADHD.

It's important for women with ADHD who are pregnant to work closely with a healthcare professional to monitor their health and the health of their developing fetus. This can include developing a treatment plan that addresses symptoms, managing stress, and closely monitoring for any potential complications. By taking a proactive approach to managing their health, women with ADHD can have a successful and healthy pregnancy.

Chapter Nine: Helpful Apps And Tools For A Wife With ADHD?

There are several phone apps available that can help women with ADHD in managing symptoms and improving daily life. Here are a few examples:

Headspace: This app provides guided meditation and mindfulness exercises to help manage stress and improve focus.

Trello: This app is a virtual to-do list that can help with organization and time management, making it easier to stay on top of tasks.

Forest: This app provides a gamified way to improve focus by planting virtual trees that grow when the user avoids distractions.

Habitica: This app turns daily tasks into a game, providing rewards for completing tasks and penalties for not completing them.

Cozi: This app helps with family organization, providing a shared calendar, grocery lists, and other tools to keep track of family activities and schedules.

Focus@Will: This app provides personalized background music designed to improve focus and concentration.

MindShift: This app provides strategies and tools for managing anxiety, a common co-occurring condition with ADHD.

Check out 25 Mobile Apps for ADHD Mind.

Planner: A planner can help individuals with ADHD to keep track of their appointments, tasks, and deadlines. It can help them to plan their day, set goals, and prioritize tasks. By breaking down tasks into smaller, manageable steps, individuals with ADHD can feel less overwhelmed and more in control of their schedule. Additionally, using a planner can help them to develop a sense of routine and structure, which can be beneficial in managing their symptoms.

Workbook: A workbook can provide individuals with ADHD with strategies and tools for managing their symptoms. It can help them to identify their strengths and weaknesses, set goals, and develop coping skills. By working through exercises and activities in a workbook, individuals with ADHD can develop a better understanding of their symptoms and how to manage them.

Journal: A journal can be a helpful tool for individuals with ADHD to process their thoughts and emotions. It can provide a space to reflect on their experiences, identify patterns in their behaviour, and track their progress. By writing down their thoughts and feelings, individuals with ADHD can develop a greater sense of self-awareness and improve their emotional regulation.

Overall, using a planner, workbook, or journal can be beneficial for individuals with ADHD in managing their symptoms and improving their daily functioning. It is important to note that while these tools can be helpful, they may not be sufficient on their own, and individuals with

ADHD may also benefit from medication, therapy, or other forms of support.

Chapter Ten: Self-Care For Women With ADHD

Self-care is an important aspect of managing ADHD symptoms, and there are several options available for women with ADHD. Here are a few self-care options that can be helpful for managing ADHD:

Exercise: Regular physical activity can help improve focus and reduce symptoms of ADHD.

Sleep: Getting enough sleep is important for managing ADHD symptoms, so establishing good sleep habits can be helpful. This includes setting a regular bedtime and avoiding caffeine and electronics before bedtime.

Nutrition: Eating a balanced diet with plenty of whole foods, healthy fats, and protein can help manage ADHD symptoms.

Mindfulness practices: Meditation, yoga, or other mindfulness practices can help improve focus, manage stress, and regulate emotions.

Hobbies: Engaging in enjoyable hobbies or creative activities can help improve mood and provide a sense of accomplishment.

Self-reflection: Taking time to reflect on your thoughts and emotions can help with emotional regulation and self-awareness.

Self-care is just one part of managing ADHD, and women with ADHD should work closely with a healthcare professional to develop a comprehensive treatment plan that addresses their specific needs and challenges. By incorporating a variety of strategies and techniques, women with ADHD can successfully manage their symptoms and improve their quality of life.

How to Destigmatize ADHD

Dr. Archer possesses a unique perspective on ADHD as he not only has the condition but has also never used medication to manage it. With the help of new scientific knowledge and research, he aims to promote public interest and initiate debates through his optimistic approach. His objective is to guide the millions of people around the world with ADHD towards a better understanding and recognition of their numerous strengths and innate potential.

There are several ways to destigmatize ADHD and raise awareness about the condition. Here are a few strategies:

Education: Providing accurate and accessible information about ADHD can help reduce misconceptions and stigma. This can include sharing information through social media, community events, and other public platforms.

Advocacy: Advocating for policies and practices that support individuals with ADHD can help reduce stigma and increase access to resources and support. This can include advocating for better access to mental health care, accommodations in school and workplace settings, and policies that reduce discrimination.

Personal stories: Sharing personal stories about living with ADHD can help increase understanding and empathy for those with the condition. This can include sharing personal experiences through social media, blogs, or other platforms.

Positive messaging: Using positive messaging and language to talk about ADHD can help reduce stigma and promote acceptance. This can include reframing ADHD as a neurodivergent trait rather than a disorder.

Cultural change: Changing cultural attitudes about ADHD can help reduce stigma in the long term. This can include promoting diversity and inclusion in media representation, education, and public discourse.

By raising awareness about ADHD and advocating for policies and practices that support individuals with the condition, we can work to reduce stigma and promote acceptance and inclusion.

A diagnosis of ADHD doesn't have to be a reason to give up on achieving one's goals. It's not the end of the world nor an excuse for not accomplishing anything. There are several inspiring stories of celebrities who have ADHD and have gone on to achieve great success in their lives despite the challenges they face.

Karina Smirnoff

Karina Smirnoff is a professional dancer and performer who is best known for her appearances on the hit television show "Dancing with the Stars." She went public with her ADHD diagnosis in 2009 and has since become an advocate for greater understanding and acceptance of the disorder.

Despite the challenges of managing her symptoms, Smirnoff has been able to achieve great success in her career thanks in part to her ability to channel her energy into her dancing. She has won numerous championships and awards throughout her career, including five U.S. National Championships and a World Trophy Championship.

Smirnoff has also been active in raising awareness about ADHD and advocating for greater support and resources for those living with the disorder. She has spoken publicly about her experiences and has encouraged others to seek help and support if they are struggling with ADHD.

Through her work as a dancer and advocate, Karina Smirnoff has shown that it is possible to achieve great things even in the face of significant challenges. Her story serves as an inspiration to others living with ADHD and other neurological disorders, reminding them that they too can succeed and thrive with the right support and resources.

Paris Hilton

Paris Hilton, the socialite and hotel heiress, disclosed in an interview with Larry King that she had been diagnosed with ADD as a child and has been taking medication for it ever since. "Since I have ADD, I have been on medication for it since my childhood," she stated.

Simone Biles

Simone Biles is an American gymnast who has won numerous medals and accolades for her outstanding performance in gymnastics. She rose to fame during the 2016 Olympics, where she won several gold medals and captured the hearts of millions of fans around the world.

In 2018, it was revealed that Biles had tested positive for methylphenidate, a drug commonly used to treat attention deficit hyperactivity disorder (ADHD). Biles, who has been open about her ADHD diagnosis, confirmed that she had been taking medication for the disorder since she was a child.

Despite the positive test, Biles was not penalized by the Olympic committee, as the use of methylphenidate is permitted under certain conditions. Biles reiterated her commitment to fair play and clean sport, emphasizing that she had always followed the rules and would continue to do so.

Biles has since continued to compete at the highest level of gymnastics, and her success has inspired many others who struggle with ADHD and other challenges to pursue their dreams and passions. She has also become an advocate for mental health, speaking out about the importance of self-care and seeking help when needed.

Solange Knowles

Solange Knowles, a singer, songwriter, and artist, initially did not find comfort in receiving a diagnosis of ADHD. In fact, she sought a second opinion from another doctor. After being diagnosed twice, she realized that ADHD is a real medical condition and noticed many symptoms of the disorder in people within the music industry. Despite the challenges associated with ADHD, Solange and other celebrities have shown that individuals with this condition can lead fulfilling lives. Finding a personalized treatment plan is crucial in managing ADHD symptoms, and sticking to the plan can help individuals thrive.

Taking Advantage Of The Situation

"YOUR ADHD MAY MAKE THINGS HARDER, BUT IT DOESN'T MAKE YOU ANY LESS CAPABLE. YOU ARE STRONG, SMART, AND RESILIENT, AND YOU CAN ACHIEVE ANYTHING YOU SET YOUR MIND TO."

While the symptoms and challenges associated with ADHD can be difficult to manage, there are also some potential strengths and "superpowers" that can come along with the condition.

For women specifically, here are a few potential superpowers that can come with ADHD:

Hyperfocus: While individuals with ADHD may struggle with focusing on tasks they find uninteresting or challenging, they can also experience intense focus on tasks they find engaging or stimulating. This can lead to a high level of productivity and creativity, as well as the ability to work on projects for extended periods without getting distracted.

Intuition: Women with ADHD often have strong intuition and the ability to sense and understand the emotions and needs of others. This can make them natural caregivers and excellent friends and partners.

Multitasking: Women with ADHD often have the ability to multitask and juggle multiple responsibilities at once. While this can be challenging at times, it can also be a superpower in environments that require rapid task-switching and quick decision-making.

Creativity: ADHD has been linked to increased creativity and out-of-the-box thinking. Women with ADHD often have unique ideas and approaches to problem-solving that can lead to innovative solutions and breakthroughs.

It's important to note that not all women with ADHD will have these specific strengths or abilities and that ADHD can also come with a range of challenges and difficulties. However, by recognizing and harnessing these potential superpowers, women with ADHD can work towards achieving their goals and living fulfilling lives.

Chapter Eleven: Helping ADHD Wife With Daily Tasks.

Household chores are the things women are naturally good at. But it's not the case with women with ADHD. Living with ADHD can make daily tasks, such as cooking and cleaning, challenging and overwhelming for some individuals. Here are some strategies that might be helpful in making these tasks more manageable and convenient for your ADHD wife:

Create a routine and stick to it: Individuals with ADHD often thrive on structure and routine. Help your wife establish a regular schedule for cooking and cleaning that works for both of you. This can include designating specific days for certain tasks or setting a regular time each day to complete them.

Make a to-do list: Creating a to-do list can help your wife stay organized and on-task. Make a list of the cooking and cleaning tasks that need to be completed each day or week and have your wife check them off as she completes them.

Break tasks into smaller steps: Large tasks, such as cleaning the entire house or cooking a multi-course meal, can be overwhelming for someone with ADHD. Help your wife break down these tasks into smaller, more manageable steps.

Minimize distractions: ADHD can make it difficult to stay focused. Try to minimize distractions in the environment while your wife is cooking or cleaning. This might mean turning off the TV or asking other family members to keep noise levels down.

Use visual cues: Visual cues can be helpful for individuals with ADHD. Consider using color-coded labels or signs to help your wife find and organize items in the kitchen or around the house.

Get organized: A cluttered and disorganized environment can be overwhelming for someone with ADHD. Help your wife get organized by creating designated spaces for kitchen tools and supplies, and finding ways to streamline the cleaning process, such as using a cleaning caddy to keep supplies together.

Use timers: Set a timer for each cleaning task to help stay focused and avoid getting sidetracked.

Use multi-purpose cleaning products: Using multi-purpose cleaning products can help simplify the cleaning process and reduce the number of products needed. Products like all-purpose cleaners, disinfecting wipes, and microfiber cloths can be used for a variety of surfaces and tasks.

Invest in cleaning tools that make the job easier: Using tools like a cordless vacuum or a robotic vacuum can help make cleaning easier and less time-consuming. Other tools like a squeegee for cleaning glass surfaces or a Swiffer for quick floor cleaning can also be helpful.

Use natural cleaning products: For women with ADHD who may be sensitive to chemical smells or want to avoid harsh chemicals, using natural cleaning products can be a good option. Products like vinegar, baking soda, and lemon juice can be used to clean a variety of surfaces and are safe for the environment.

Involve others: Asking for help from family members or roommates can make cleaning tasks less overwhelming and more manageable.

Reward yourself: Celebrate completing a cleaning task by treating yourself to something you enjoy, like a favorite snack or activity. This can help motivate you to continue with your cleaning routine.

Consider professional help: If your wife continues to struggle with cooking and cleaning despite your best efforts, consider seeking the help of a professional. A therapist or ADHD coach can provide individualized strategies to help your wife manage her symptoms and develop effective coping strategies.

Is ADHD hereditary?

Yes, ADHD has a significant genetic component and is known to run in families. Research has shown that there is a hereditary link to ADHD and that children with a parent or sibling with ADHD are more likely to develop the condition themselves. In fact, studies suggest that genetics may account for up to 70-80% of the risk for developing ADHD, while environmental factors may contribute to the remaining risk.

However, it's important to note that having a genetic predisposition for ADHD does not necessarily mean that an individual will develop the condition. Environmental factors, such as exposure to toxins or stress, can also contribute to the development of ADHD. Additionally, there may be genetic factors that interact with environmental factors to increase the risk of developing ADHD.

If you have a family history of ADHD or suspect that you may have the condition, it's important to speak with a healthcare professional for evaluation and potential treatment. Early identification and intervention can help improve outcomes and reduce the impact of ADHD on daily life.

Chapter Twelve: Comorbid Conditions

Comorbid conditions are associated disorders that come along with other ADHD symptoms. Because of their past experiences, many individuals with ADHD also exhibit anxiety or hypersensitivity. CBT makes it simple to address other critical concerns that affect ADHD symptoms, such as co-occurring mood and anxiety disorders and hyperfocus on technology. Because the approaches used to treat each illness differ, it may be preferable for you and your therapist to focus on one at a time before moving on to the next. Remember that none of these conditions will go away on their own. They all necessitate practice, awareness, and the challenge of negative beliefs.

Some of the most common comorbid conditions with ADHD include:

Anxiety disorders: Individuals with ADHD may also experience anxiety disorders such as generalized anxiety disorder, panic disorder, social anxiety disorder, or obsessive-compulsive disorder.

Mood disorders: Depression and bipolar disorder are common comorbidities with ADHD, particularly in adults.

Learning disabilities: Many people with ADHD also have learning disabilities, such as dyslexia, dysgraphia, or dyscalculia.

Autism spectrum disorders: ADHD may co-occur with autism spectrum disorders, particularly in children.

Substance use disorders: Individuals with ADHD are at an increased risk of developing substance use disorders, such as alcohol or drug addiction.

Sleep disorders: Sleep disorders, such as insomnia, sleep apnea, or restless leg syndrome, are more common in individuals with ADHD.

Tourette's syndrome: ADHD can also occur with Tourette's syndrome, which is a neurological disorder characterized by repetitive, involuntary movements and vocalizations.

Not all individuals with ADHD will experience these comorbid conditions, and not all individuals with these conditions will also have ADHD.

Why ADHD Brain Chooses Less Important Tasks

People with ADHD may have difficulty focusing on tasks, organizing their thoughts, and completing tasks in a timely manner. As a result, they may appear to choose less important tasks or get distracted by non-essential activities.

One reason for this may be that the ADHD brain is less able to filter out distractions and focus on important tasks. Research has shown that people with ADHD have differences in the structure and function of certain areas of the brain that are involved in attention, working memory, and decision-making. These differences can make it harder for people with ADHD to prioritize tasks and stay on task.

Additionally, people with ADHD may have difficulties with motivation and goal-setting. They may struggle to prioritize tasks that they don't find interesting or rewarding or have trouble breaking down large tasks into smaller, more manageable steps. This can lead to procrastination or avoidance of important tasks.

It's important to note that everyone, regardless of whether or not they have ADHD, can struggle with prioritizing tasks or getting distracted by less important activities. However, for people with ADHD, these challenges can be more pronounced and have a significant impact on their daily lives. Treatment for ADHD typically involves a combination of medication, behavioural therapy, and accommodations to help manage symptoms and improve daily functioning.

Helpful Mantras For People With ADHD?

Mantras can be a helpful tool for individuals with ADHD to improve focus and manage symptoms. A mantra is a word or phrase that is repeated to help promote a sense of calm and focus. Here are some examples of mantras that may be helpful for individuals with ADHD:

"Stay present": This mantra can help individuals with ADHD focus on the present moment and avoid distractions.

"One thing at a time": This mantra can help individuals with ADHD avoid feeling overwhelmed by focusing on one task at a time.

"I am capable": This mantra can help individuals with ADHD build confidence in their abilities and avoid negative self-talk.

"Breathe": This mantra can help individuals with ADHD remember to take deep breaths and relax when feeling stressed or overwhelmed.

"Progress, not perfection": This mantra can help individuals with ADHD avoid getting bogged down in details and focus on making progress, rather than achieving perfection.

Remember, mantras are a personal choice and what works for one person may not work for another. It's important to find a mantra that resonates with you and use it.

Eating Disorder In Girls

According to the study, "Are girls with ADHD at risk for eating disorders?" by Biederman et al. (2007), girls with ADHD are at increased risk for developing eating disorders, particularly bulimia nervosa. The study found that girls with ADHD were five times more likely to develop bulimia nervosa compared to girls without ADHD. The study also found a higher prevalence of binge eating disorder and purging disorder among girls with ADHD. The authors suggest that the impulsivity and emotional dysregulation associated with ADHD may contribute to the development of eating disorders in this population.

Chapter Thirteen: Ineffective Parenting

The article "Parental ADHD symptomatology and ineffective parenting: The connecting link of home chaos" published in the journal Parenting in 2010, explores the link between parental ADHD symptoms and ineffective parenting, mediated by the presence of home chaos.

The authors argue that parental ADHD symptoms can interfere with effective parenting practices, such as providing clear and consistent rules, routines, and consequences for children's behaviour. This can lead to increased home chaos, which refers to a disorganized and unpredictable home environment characterized by clutter, noise, and lack of structure.

The study used a sample of 124 parents with children aged 6-12 years, and assessed parental ADHD symptoms, parenting practices, home chaos, and child behaviour problems through self-report questionnaires. The results showed that parental ADHD symptoms were associated with more home chaos, which in turn increased child behaviour problems.

Furthermore, the study found that the relationship between parental ADHD symptoms and child behaviour problems was mediated by home chaos, indicating that home chaos is a key connecting link between parental ADHD symptoms and ineffective parenting practices.

The authors suggest that interventions targeting both parental ADHD symptoms and home chaos may be effective in improving parenting practices and reducing child behaviour problems. They also highlight the importance of raising awareness among parents with ADHD about the potential impact of their symptoms on parenting practices and the need for support and resources to manage these challenges.

Overall, the study emphasizes the complex and interconnected nature of ADHD symptoms, parenting practices, and home chaos, and highlights the need for a comprehensive and holistic approach to addressing these issues in families affected by ADHD.

Difference Between ADHD And ASD

ADHD (Attention-Deficit/Hyperactivity Disorder) and ASD (Autism Spectrum Disorder) are two separate neurodevelopmental disorders that affect behaviour, cognition, and social communication, but they differ in several key ways.

Core Symptoms: ADHD is primarily characterized by symptoms of inattention, hyperactivity, and impulsivity, while ASD is primarily characterized by difficulties in social interaction, communication, and restricted, repetitive patterns of behaviour, interests, or activities.

Onset: ADHD symptoms typically begin in childhood, while ASD symptoms may be apparent in early childhood or emerge later during development.

Cognitive Abilities: While individuals with ADHD may have difficulties with executive function (e.g. planning, organizing, and regulating behaviour), their overall intellectual abilities are typically within the normal range. In contrast, individuals with ASD may have a range of cognitive abilities, from intellectual disability to above-average intelligence.

Social Communication: While individuals with ADHD may struggle with social skills due to impulsivity or distractibility, they do not typically have the social communication difficulties that are characteristic of ASD.

Sensory Sensitivities: Individuals with ASD often experience sensory sensitivities (e.g. hypersensitivity to certain sounds or textures) while individuals with ADHD may not experience these types of sensory issues.

Co-occurring Conditions: Both ADHD and ASD are often accompanied by other conditions such as anxiety, depression, and sleep disorders, but ADHD is more commonly associated with these co-occurring conditions.

It's important to note that while ADHD and ASD have distinct differences, they can also overlap and co-occur in some individuals. A comprehensive evaluation by a qualified healthcare provider is necessary to determine an accurate diagnosis and develop an appropriate treatment plan.

The article "Psychopathology in females with attention-deficit/hyperactivity disorder" was published in the Journal of Attention Disorders in 2006. The authors of the article are Ellen B. Littman and Patricia K. Pueschel.

The article examines the prevalence and types of psychopathology that are associated with ADHD in females. The authors note that while ADHD is commonly thought of as a disorder that primarily affects males, it is also prevalent in females. However, because the diagnostic criteria for ADHD are based on male behaviour patterns, many females with ADHD may be undiagnosed or misdiagnosed.

The authors reviewed the literature on ADHD in females and found that females with ADHD often have comorbid disorders such as anxiety, depression, and eating disorders. They also note that females with ADHD are more likely to internalize their symptoms, which can lead to difficulties with self-esteem and self-worth.

The authors suggest that clinicians who work with females with ADHD should be aware of the high rates of comorbid disorders and the different presentations of ADHD in females.

They also suggest that treatment approaches should be tailored to the individual and should address both ADHD symptoms and any comorbid disorders.

Overall, the article highlights the need for greater awareness and understanding of ADHD in females and the importance of accurate diagnosis and appropriate treatment for females with ADHD.

Here's some information on both studies:

"Psychopathology in females with attention-deficit/hyperactivity disorder, five-year prospective study" (2006):
This study aimed to investigate the long-term psychiatric outcomes in females with ADHD. The researchers followed up with 140 girls with ADHD and 122 control subjects over a period of five years. They found that the girls with ADHD were more likely to have anxiety disorders, depression, and oppositional defiant disorder than the control group.

The study highlights the importance of early detection and treatment of ADHD in females to prevent long-term psychiatric comorbidities. The study was published in the Journal of the American Academy of Child and Adolescent Psychiatry.

"Evidence-based guidelines for the pharmacological management of attention deficit hyperactivity disorder" (2014):
This study aimed to develop evidence-based guidelines for the pharmacological management of ADHD. The researchers conducted a systematic review of the literature to identify randomized controlled trials of pharmacological treatments for ADHD.

They then synthesized the evidence to develop guidelines for the use of medications such as stimulants, non-stimulants, and alpha-agonists in the treatment of ADHD. The guidelines provide clinicians with evidence-based recommendations for the selection, dosing, and monitoring of medications for the treatment of ADHD. The study was published in the Journal of the American Academy of Child and Adolescent Psychiatry.

ADHD Communication Game

Here's a game that can be played by an ADHD partner and their non-ADHD partner to help improve communication and understanding between them:

Title: "Find the Balance"

Objective: The objective of the game is to improve communication and understanding between an ADHD partner and a non-ADHD partner. The game is designed to help the non-ADHD partner better understand the unique challenges faced by their ADHD partner and to help the ADHD partner develop better-coping strategies.

Gameplay:

Choose a quiet and comfortable environment to play the game. Turn off all distractions such as TV, radio, and cell phones.

Have the non-ADHD partner begin by sharing a recent experience where they felt frustrated or misunderstood by their ADHD partner.

The ADHD partner should then share a recent experience where they felt overwhelmed or struggled to focus.

Both partners should take turns sharing their perspectives and feelings about each other's experiences.

After each partner shares their experience, they should work together to brainstorm ways to improve communication and understanding in the future.

The non-ADHD partner should try to provide positive reinforcement and support for their ADHD partner, while the ADHD partner should try to actively listen and be receptive to feedback.

Repeat the process for as many rounds as desired, with each partner taking turns sharing their experiences and working together to find solutions.

Winning the game:

The objective of the game is not to win or lose, but to improve communication and understanding between the partners. However, the game can be considered a success if both partners feel more connected and have a better understanding of each other's perspectives and needs.

Benefits:

Playing "Find the Balance" can help improve communication and understanding between partners, which can lead to a stronger relationship. The game can also help the ADHD partner develop better-coping strategies and reduce the risk of misunderstandings and conflicts.

REFERENCES

The article "Psychopathology in females with attention-deficit/hyperactivity disorder" was published in the Journal of Attention Disorders in 2006. The authors of the article are Ellen B. Littman and Patricia K. Pueschel.

(2014) Evidence-based guidelines for the pharmacological management of attention deficit hyperactivity disorder

Anker E, Bendiksen B & Heir, T (2018) Comorbid psychiatric disorders in a clinical sample of adults with ADHD

Biederman J, Ball, SW & Monuteaux MC (2007) Are girls with ADHD at risk for eating disorders

Brevik, EJ, Lundervold, AJ, Halmoy A et al (2017) Prevalence and clinical correlates of insomnia in adults with attention-deficit hyperactivity disorder

Antshel KM, Zhang-James, Y & Faraone SV (2013) The comorbidity of ADHD and an autism spectrum disorder. Expert

Brown, NM (2020) Childhood trauma and ADHD: A complete overview and clinical guide.

Quinn PO & Madhoo M (2014) A review of attention-deficit/hyperactivity disorder in women and girls: Uncovering
this hidden diagnosis. Prim Care Companion CNS Disord, 16(3).

Royal College of Psychiatrists (2021) Attention deficit hyperactivity disorder (ADHD) in adults with intellectual disability
CR230, Feb 2021.
Rucklidge JJ, Tannock R (2001) Psychiatric, psychosocial, and cognitive functioning of female adolescents with
ADHD.

J Am Acad Child Adolesc Psychiatry,

Rusting, R (2018) Decoding the overlap between autism and ADHD

Young, S & Bramham, J (2012) Cognitive-behavioral therapy for ADHD in adolescents and adults: A Psychological Guide to Practice (2nd edition).

Conners CK, Erhardt D, Epstein JN, et al (1999) Self-ratings of ADHD symptoms in adults

Larsson, H, Chang, Z, D'Onofrio, BM, et al (2014) The heritability of clinically diagnosed attention deficit hyperactivity
disorder across the lifespan. Psychol Med, 44(10):2223–29.

Parental ADHD symptomatology and ineffective parenting: The connecting
link of home chaos. Parenting, 10(2):119–35. DOI: 10.1080/15295190903212844

NICE (2018) Attention deficit hyperactivity disorder: Diagnosis and management (NG87). National Institute for Health
and Care Excellence.

Nutt DJ, Fone K, Asherson P et al (2007) Evidence-based guidelines for the management of attention-deficit/hyperactivity
disorder in adolescents in transition to adult services and in adults: Recommendations from the British Association
for Psychopharmacology. Journal of Psychopharmacology, 21:10–41.

Quinn PO & Madhoo M (2014) A review of attention-deficit/hyperactivity disorder in women and girls: Uncovering
this hidden diagnosis. Prim Care Companion CNS Disord, 16(3).

Royal College of Psychiatrists (2021) Attention deficit hyperactivity disorder (ADHD) in adults with intellectual disability

CR230, Feb 2021.

Rucklidge JJ, Tannock R (2001) Psychiatric, psychosocial, and cognitive functioning of female adolescents with ADHD.

J Am Acad Child Adolesc Psychiatry,
Rusting, R (2018) Decoding the overlap between autism and ADHD

Young, S & Bramham, J (2012) Cognitive-behavioral therapy for ADHD in adolescents and adults: A Psychological Guide to Practice (2nd edition).

A Different Way of Thinking (2005) by Lynn Weiss, PhD.

Women with Attention Deficit Disorder: Embrace Your Differences and Transform Your Life (2012) by Sari Solden, MS, MFCC
Help for Women with ADHD: My Simple Strategies for Conquering Chaos (2017) by Joan Wilder

Journeys Through ADulthood: Discover a New Sense of Identity and Meaning While Living with Attention Deficit Disorder (2004) by Sari Solden, MS, MFCC

25 Mobile Apps
https://www.additudemag.com/mobile-apps-for-adhd-minds/

Made in United States
Troutdale, OR
01/07/2024